J. K. ROWLING

Gloria D. Miklowitz

DOMINIE PRESS
Pearson Learning Group

Publisher: Raymond Yuen
Editor: Bob Rowland
Designer: Greg DiGenti
Photo Credits: Graham Barclay /Corbis (cover and Page 18); Murdo MacLeod/Corbis (Page 11); Reuters/Corbis (pages 25 and 31); and Tim Graham/Corbis (Page 34)

Text copyright © 2005 Gloria D. Miklowitz

All rights reserved. No part of this publication may be reproduced or transmitted in any form or by any means without permission in writing from the publisher. Reproduction of any part of this book, through photocopy, recording, or any electronic or mechanical retrieval system, without the written permission of the publisher, is an infringement of the copyright law.

Published by:

Dominie Press, Inc.

1949 Kellogg Avenue
Carlsbad, California 92008 USA

www.dominie.com

Paperback ISBN 0-7685-3048-2
Library Bound Edition ISBN 0-7685-3575-1
Printed in Singapore by PH Productions Pte Ltd
2 3 4 5 PH 07 06 05

Table of Contents

Chapter 1
A Writer from the Start...........5

Chapter 2
The "Birth" of Harry Potter...............9

Chapter 3
Finally, a Finished Manuscript!
But Would Anyone Publish It? 15

Chapter 4
***Harry* Goes to Press** 22

Chapter 5
A Word of Advice 27

Glossary 35

Chapter 1

A Writer from the Start

J. K. Rowling wrote her first story, called *Rabbit*, when she was just six years old. Years later, unable to afford a typewriter, she wrote short stories and half-finished novels by hand. When she finally completed her first manuscript, publishers told her it was "too long," "too slow," and "too literary."

That manuscript, titled *Harry Potter and the Philosopher's Stone*, would eventually sell millions of copies in more than 200 countries, win literary awards, and capture readers' imaginations all over the world.

"I thought I'd written something that only a handful of people might like, so this has been something of a shock," said Joanne Kathleen Rowling, known to her many fans as J. K. Rowling.

⚡

J. K. was born on July 31, 1965 in the tiny town of Chipping Sodbury, England. Her mother, Ann, worked as a technician. Her father, Peter, was an aircraft factory manager. The Rowlings were loving parents. Their house was filled with books, and they read constantly—fairy tales, fantasies, and the classics.

"My most vivid memory of childhood is my father reading *The Wind in the Willows* to me," J. K. told the *Daily Telegraph* in London. "I had the measles at the time, but I don't really remember that," she said. "I just remember the book."

When she was almost two years old, her sister, Di, was born. J. K. began making up stories to tell her. Both children wanted a rabbit, but they weren't allowed to have one. As a result, J. K.'s stories were often about rabbits, with Di as the heroine of each tale.

When she was six, J. K. wrote down one of her stories. It was about Rabbit with measles, and Rabbit's friends, including a giant bee named Miss Bee, who came to visit. J. K. said later, "Ever since Rabbit and Miss Bee, I wanted to be a writer. I cannot overstate how much I wanted that." But she rarely told anyone about her dream.

Over the next few years, J. K.'s family moved several times. In one town where they lived, she became friends with a boy and girl named Ian and Vikki Potter. The children liked to dress up and make up stories. Years later, J. K. would choose "Potter" as Harry's last name.

Chapter 2

The "Birth" of Harry Potter

When J. K. was nine, her family moved again, this time to Tutshill, a small village with a forest and river nearby and fields all around to play in. All through her school years J. K.'s happiest times involved reading a book or writing. She especially loved books by Jane Austen and the C.S. Lewis *Narnia* series, *The Chronicles of Narnia*. For pets, she and her sister, Di, had a dog named Misty. J. K. wore glasses as a child. They were "like bottle bottoms," she said. "That's why Harry wears glasses."

After elementary school J. K. attended Wyedean Comprehensive, similar to high school in the United States. English was her favorite subject. She would entertain friends at lunchtime with stories she invented. Even though she continued to secretly write, she didn't show her stories to others. She graduated from Wyedean with high honors. Her teachers believed she had a bright future.

When she was eighteen, J. K. was uncertain what to do next. She had boxes of stories she had written, but

Photo portrait of British author J. K. Rowling

how could she get them published? And were they even good enough to be published? The best thing to do, her parents believed, was for her to go to Exeter University and major in French. With a degree in French, she could earn a living as a bilingual secretary. It wasn't what she wanted to do, but she agreed. She attended Exeter for four years, including one year teaching English in France. Now it was time to earn a living.

Over the next six years, J. K. worked in a number of secretarial jobs. "I proved to be the worst secretary ever," she once said. Whatever job she held, she often spent lunch hours at coffee shops or cafés, sitting in a corner, writing. Instead of taking notes at meetings, as she was expected to do, she was often busy jotting down new story and character ideas.

"I was writing a lot of short stories and a lot of started and abandoned novels," she told the School Library Journal. Those works wound up in boxes with all the other stories she never sent out to publishers.

In a very real sense, Harry Potter was "born" on a train in 1990. At the time, J. K. was unsure where her life was going. She had taken a new job with the Manchester Chamber of Commerce and traveled there from London by train every day. One day, on her way back to London, the train broke down. The passengers were told that repairs would take four hours. J. K. was staring out the window at some cows, when suddenly the idea for Harry Potter came to her.

"Harry just strolled into my head fully formed," she said. "I can't tell you why or what triggered it. But I saw the idea of Harry and the wizard school very plainly. I suddenly had this basic idea of a boy who didn't know what he was."

Without a pen or paper for writing, she sat quietly, thinking about characters for the story, unusual names, and dramatic, magical scenes. By the time the train reached London, J. K. had much of the plan for the first Harry Potter book mapped out in her head.

Chapter 3

Finally, a Finished Manuscript!
But Would Anyone Publish It?

While she was working for the Manchester Chamber of Commerce, J. K. used every spare minute to fill in details of *Harry Potter and the Philosopher's Stone*. While she was working on that first book, her mother died suddenly of multiple sclerosis. She was forty-five years old. J. K. loved her mother very much, and she felt guilty because she hadn't been with her during her last hours—and because she hadn't shared her writing with her. She told *People* magazine that the only thing that got her through that difficult time was writing about Harry Potter.

Once again, J. K. felt as though she was drifting. She had lost her mother, and her job was going nowhere. She decided to give up secretarial work and go abroad to teach English in Oporto, Portugal.

At first J. K. missed her family and friends, but soon she came to love the climate, the city of Oporto, and the way of life in Portugal. She taught in the afternoons and evenings, but she was free to write in the mornings.

It was during this period that J. K. fell in love with, and eventually married, a television journalist. J. K. remembers that as a happy period in her life. She taught classes and wrote, developing more and more of Harry Potter. She could see ahead to future books continuing Harry's adventures. J. K.'s daughter, Jessica, was born in 1993, but J. K. became very depressed. Her husband was too often away on assignments, and although she loved her baby, she felt like "a nonperson" who needed to achieve something. Soon, her marriage ended, and she couldn't seem to get back to writing.

Her sister, Di, urged her to come to Edinburgh, Scotland, where she and other family members lived. J. K. packed up baby Jessica and the early chapters of *Harry Potter and the Sorcerer's Stone*

J. K. Rowling, creator of the adventures of Harry Potter, surrounded by her first love—books

and left Portugal to join Di and the others in Edinburgh.

"I had a tiny baby, no job, and I was in a strange place," J. K. told *People* magazine. She didn't want to apply for welfare. After all, she was a college graduate and had job skills. But how else could she finish the Harry Potter book and pay for rent and food?

A friend loaned her enough money to rent a small, cold, dismal room. One dreary day, while visiting Di, J. K. told her about the book she'd been writing. Di insisted on reading it, and she loved what she read!

Encouraged by Di's positive response, J. K. made a pact with herself. She would give herself one year to finish the book. Meanwhile, she applied for public assistance. The money barely covered the cost of rent and food, and some nights she went to bed hungry.

Every day, except when the weather was very bad, J. K. pushed Jessica in a stroller until the baby fell asleep. Then, she would go to a nearby café and sit at a table, with a cup of coffee—and write. "She was quite an odd sight," the co-owner of Nicolson's Café said. She would "push the pram with one hand and write away." J. K. couldn't even afford a used typewriter, so she wrote by hand on scraps of paper.

Day after day the story grew. Harry, Hermione, and Ron became as alive to J. K. as real people. She laughed at the names she made up, like Professor Dumbledore and Hagrid. And she was entertained by her own descriptions of how Quidditch is played. Finally, early in 1994, the book was finished. J. K. went over it again, making it as good as she could. The story was long—80,000 words —almost twice as long as most novels for young readers. She had learned that a literary agent was needed to get a book read by a publisher. She bought a used typewriter and typed two copies of the manuscript. She sent them to two agents she chose from a list at the library.

It must have felt strange to J. K. to wake up each day without writing about Harry, but now she could get a job and get off welfare. As each day passed without word about her manuscript, she worried. Would an agent want to represent her book?

Chapter 4

Harry Goes to Press

The year J. K. finished the first Harry Potter book she applied for and was given a grant from the Scottish Arts Council to help her complete *Harry Potter and the Chamber of Secrets*. The money allowed her to pay for childcare for Jessica, freeing her to go back to work that paid, teaching French. She went off welfare a year after arriving in Scotland.

Every day she rushed to the mailbox, hoping to hear from one of the literary agents. At last, a letter arrived from Christopher Little. Trembling with fear and hope, she opened the envelope. The letter read, "We would be pleased to represent your manuscript on an exclusive basis."

When she met Little, he said, "I don't want you going away from this meeting thinking you're going to make a fortune." Few children's book authors earned more than $4,000 a year. J. K. later told School Library Journal that she didn't expect to make money or become famous. "All I ever wanted was for somebody to publish Harry so I could go to bookshops and see it," she said.

Her agent began sending the manuscript to publishers. Soon, rejection letters began arriving. Editors said her book was "too long," or "too slow," or "too literary." Christopher Little wasn't worried. He believed the book was too good *not* to be published.

Meanwhile, J. K. used her spare time to begin a second Harry Potter book. While writing, she snacked and chewed bubble gum because it reminded her of when she was seven years old.

Over a year passed before her agent called to say the British publisher Bloomsbury Press wanted to publish *Harry Potter and the Philosopher's Stone*. They were offering an advance of $4,000, hardly enough to live on, but J. K. was overjoyed. "It was comparable only to having my daughter," she said.

***J. K. Rowling signs a copy of one of her
Harry Potter books for a young fan***

Before the book was published in 1997, word got around of how original and appealing it was. Publishers from all over the world began asking about it. At the annual book fair in Bologna, Italy, where foreign rights to books are sold, an auction was arranged. The publishers who offered the most money won the right to distribute *Harry Potter and the Philosopher's Stone* in their countries.

J. K. hadn't really paid much attention to what was happening outside England when her agent called her from New York with the good news.

In Bologna, the bidding for the U.S. rights to *Harry Potter and the Philosopher's Stone* kept going up. Arthur A. Levine, editorial director of Scholastic Press, wanted to buy the publication rights very much, but did he love it enough to pay $50,000, or $70,000? J. K. was an unknown author. Should he take the chance? He took a great risk and bid $100,000, the most he'd ever paid for the rights to a children's book.

Little phoned J. K. with the news and said Arthur Levine would be calling her in a few hours. "I nearly died," she said. When the call came through, Levine said, "Don't be scared." Now, there would be work to be done to make the book even better.

Chapter 5

A Word of Advice

"I attracted a lot of publicity for which I was unprepared," J. K. said after signing the Scholastic contract before *Harry Potter and the Philosopher's Stone* was published in 1997 in England.

The book follows the magical adventures of a boy wizard named Harry Potter. It was published in the United States in 1998 as *Harry Potter and the Sorcerer's Stone*.

By year's end the book had won a number of important awards, and 500,000 copies had been sold. Even adults loved the book. A friend told J. K. she'd seen a man in a suit on a train reading Harry Potter behind his newspaper.

With money no longer a worry, J. K. rented a house in Edinburgh, and she could now afford a computer. Every day, after sending Jessica off to school, J. K. sat at her favorite table in Nicolson's Café and began writing the next Harry Potter book. She still writes in longhand. "I like physically shuffling around papers," she says.

Sales figures convinced publishers that readers wanted more of Harry Potter. J. K. signed contracts to complete Harry's story in a total of seven books. The series covers seven years in Harry's life. In them, he makes friends, battles with evil powers, and attends the Hogwarts School of Witches and Wizards, where his supplies include a magic wand and an owl who delivers his mail. Throughout the series, Harry grows from a shy, fearful boy to a confident teenager. "The seventh book will be the longest because I'm going to want to say good-bye," she said. Frightened by what was expected of her, she sat down and plotted the next books.

Interviews, phone calls, speaking engagements, mail to answer, all cut into writing time and time with Jessica. Still, J. K. wrote steadily toward her deadlines. "In an ideal day I'll work six to ten hours," she told a reporter. "But now I'm fighting to get time to write. I use cafés like offices, and I try to get away from the house whenever possible."

Several years after the first Harry Potter book arrived in bookstores, there were four more in print: *Harry Potter and the Chamber of Secrets*, *Harry Potter and the Prisoner of Azkaban*, *Harry Potter and the Goblet of Fire*, and *Harry Potter and the Order of the Phoenix*.

Meanwhile, Warner Brothers won the right to make a movie of *Harry Potter and the Sorcerer's Stone*. J. K. required that she have a say in the screenplay and that the film be live action, not animated.

J. K. Rowling holds a copy of **Harry Potter and the Order of the Phoenix** *at a bookstore in Edinburgh, Scotland* ▶

HARRY POTTER
and the Order of the Phoenix

J.K. ROWLING
BLOOMSBURY

Over 40,000 children tried out for the part of Harry Potter. J. K. found herself studying children wherever she went, wondering if they looked the part and could act. Ten weeks before filming, the producer still had not found the boy to play Harry. Finally, Daniel Radcliffe, then eleven years old, arrived to audition. He looked and acted exactly as J. K. imagined Harry to be, and he got the role.

Will J. K. continue to write after she completes the Harry Potter books? Yes. She feels uncomfortable if she goes without writing for a week. The books and films have made her rich, but she doesn't spend her money on cars and castles. She gives a great deal of money to social causes. She donated $750,000 to the National Council for One-Parent Families to help single mothers. She established a Harry Potter Fund to help children in England and Africa. She wrote two books to raise millions of dollars for the fund: *Quidditch Through the Ages*, written under the name Kennilworthy Whisp, and *Fantastic Beasts and Where to Find Them*, written under the name Newt Scamander.

J. K. has both advice and encouragement for young people who aspire to be writers. "My feeling is, if you really want to do it, you will do it," she told the editor of *January Magazine*. "You *will* find the time."

And she warns young would-be authors that they shouldn't expect their work to be perfect the first time.

"You have to resign yourself to wasting lots of trees before you write anything really good," she said. "That's just how it is. It's like learning an instrument. You've got to be prepared

Queen Elizabeth II (left) visits J. K. Rowling (center) and her editor, Emma Matthewson

for hitting wrong notes occasionally, or quite a lot. That's just part of the learning process."

And her most important piece of advice? You're following it right now!

"Read a lot," J. K. said. "Reading really helps. Read anything you can get your hands on."

Glossary

Animated – made in the form of a cartoon.

Austen, Jane – (1775-1817) a British author. Her best-known book is *Pride and Prejudice.*

Bilingual – able to speak fluently in two languages.

Bologna – a city in northern Italy.

Depressed – sad; low in spirits; unhappy. Chronic depression can lead to serious psychological problems.

Dismal – drab; depressing; gloomy.

Edinburgh – the capital of Scotland.

France – a country in Western Europe between the English Channel and the Mediterranean Sea. (The capital of France is Paris.)

Grant – a gift (in the form of money or land) designed to help a person accomplish a specific goal.

Heroine – the central female character in a book or play; a woman who is admired for her bravery and accomplishments.

Lewis, C.S. – (1898-1963) a British author and essayist.

Literary Agent – a person who represents authors and their work to publishing companies.

London – the capital of England; located in the southwestern part of the country.

Manchester – a city in northwestern England.

Multiple Sclerosis – a chronic, incurable disease that leads to partial or complete paralysis.

Pact – an agreement; a promise to meet a specific goal.

Portugal – a country in southwestern Europe. (The capital of Portugal is Lisbon.)

Rejection Letter – a notice from a publishing company telling an author that a manuscript has not been accepted for publication.

Screenplay – the script and filming directions for a story being made into a motion picture.

Secretary – an employee who takes care of personal and business mail and routine paperwork for an employer or group of employers.

Television Journalist – a reporter who covers and writes the news for television rather than newspapers.

Wizard – in fiction, a person who possesses magical influence or power.